Our Brand New Baby!

written and illustrated
by
Maryann Powell Malecki

Dedicated to my husband, Clem, who is a great father and has made mothering a rewarding experience for me.

Copyright © 1980 by The Pennypress
Printed in the United States of America
Library of Congress Catalog Card Number 80 - 53693
ISBN 0-937604-06-2

Additional copies are available from the publisher: The Pennypress
1100 23rd Avenue East
Seattle, Washington 98112
Phone (206) 325-5098

Single copy - $5.95
Bulk orders - $5.00 each for
10 or more copies

Our Grand New Baby!

By Maryann Powell Malecki R.N.

Foreword

Small children often have grand expectations about the capabilities of their brother- or sister-to-be. Not only are they often dismayed by the complete helplessness of the new arrival, but they are perplexed and angered by all of the attention they receive. What's so great about a little baby anyway?

The purpose of this book is twofold. The first is to introduce the small child to the limitations of the baby as a playmate. It may also serve as a preview to the many mixed feelings he or she may experience toward the baby and help to channel these feelings in a positive direction.

The second purpose is to encourage parents to allow the child to participate in baby care as well as to make an effort to treat the older child as the special unique little person that he or she is.

This book is designed so that it can be enjoyed and understood by children of all ages. Older children may enjoy the complete text on the left, while the younger child may be attentive to the illustrations and captions alone.

Maryann P. Malecki

Also by Maryann P. Malecki

Mom and Dad and I Are Having a Baby!

Mom and Dad and I Are Having a Baby! is for the child who will be present for the birth of a sibling, or for the child who is very interested in what childbirth is really like. Written as a child might describe pregnancy and birth, it fully describes these subjects in a fascinating and non-threatening way. The sights and sounds of birth are described and illustrated accurately so as not to be alarming when actually witnessed. The price is $5.95 for a single copy; $5.00 each for 10 copies or more. They are available from The Pennypress, 1100 23rd Ave. East, Seattle, WA 98112.

We have a brand new baby! She's a girl baby and I think that she's the cutest baby in the whole wide world!

We waited for her for such a long time. Before she was born, she grew in Mom's tummy making it bigger and bigger and bigger.

We just couldn't wait to see whether it was a boy or a girl.

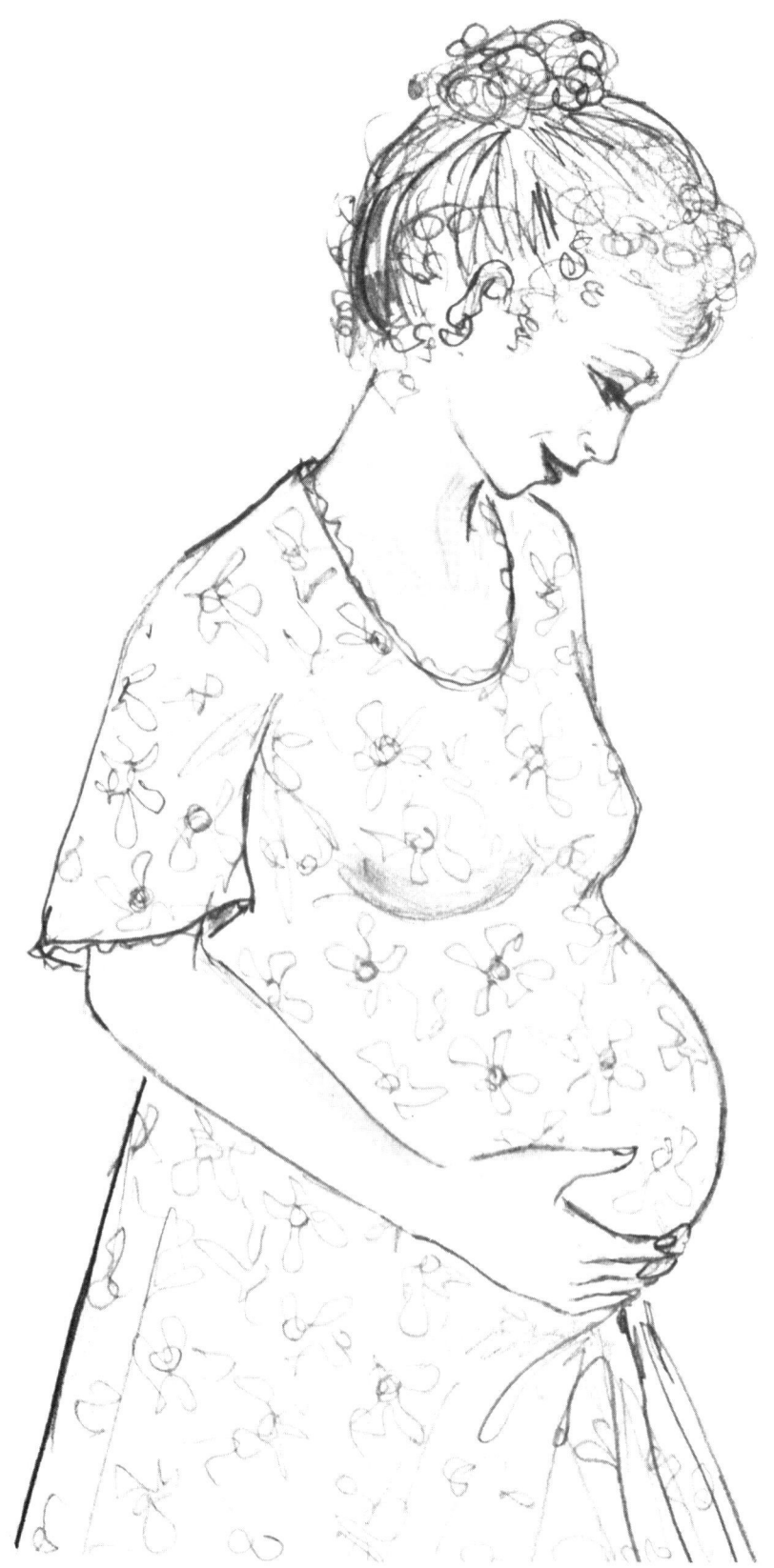

She grew in Mom's tummy, making it bigger and bigger and bigger.

Mom and I used to go to the doctor's office for baby check-ups to see if the baby in Mom's tummy was healthy.

Sometimes, I would listen to the baby's heartbeat. The doctor used a funny metal thing on his head to hear the baby, but he let me listen with my ear against Mom's tummy. If you press down hard, the baby's heartbeat sounds like a fast ticking watch. It's very hard to hear.

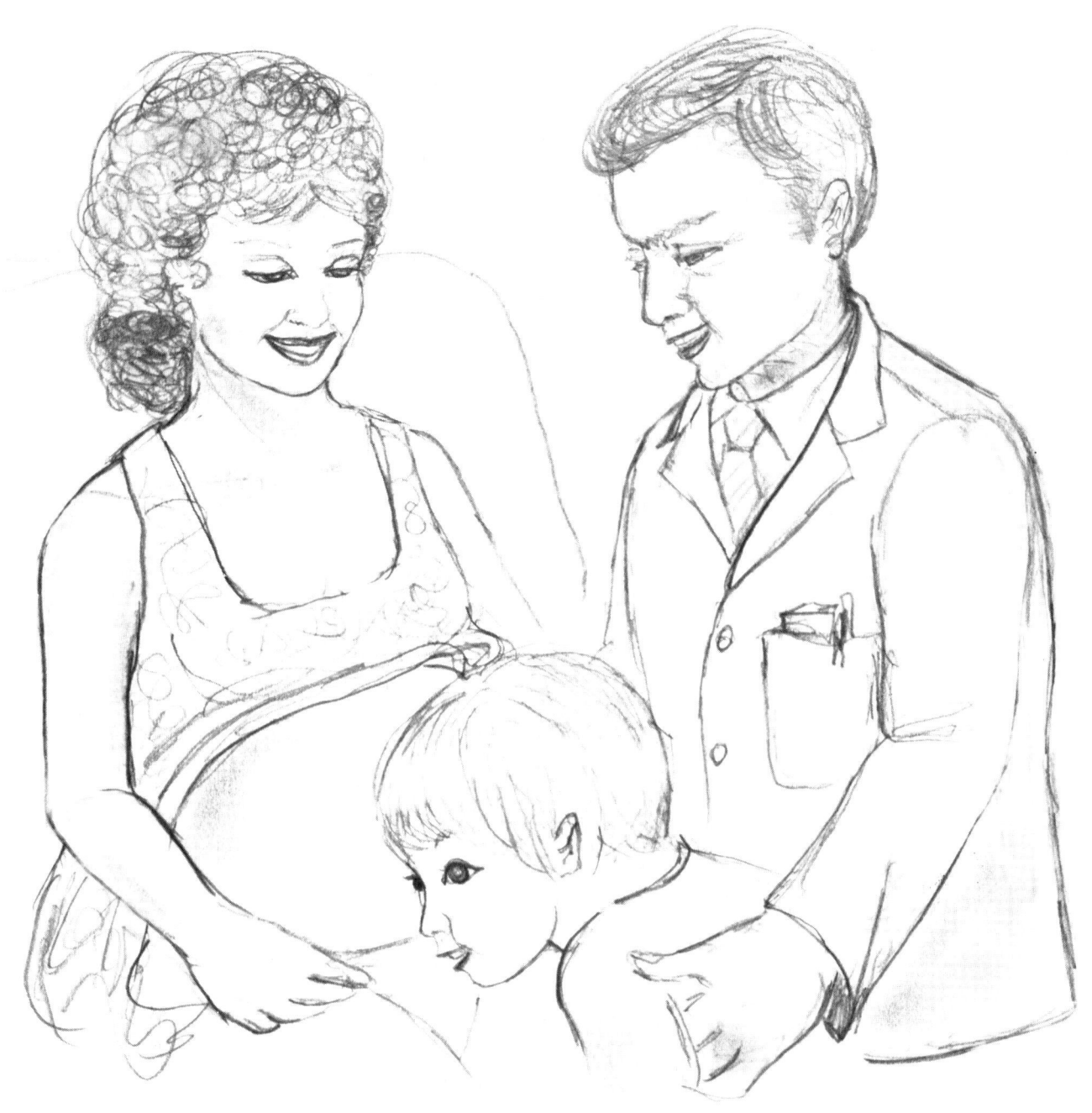

At the Doctor's office I heard the baby's heartbeat in Mom's tummy.

Lots of times, Dad and I would feel the baby kick inside of Mom's tummy. It felt real weird.

Once in awhile the baby would move all around when we were feeling her. Sometimes we could even see her move. That always made Mom smile.

Dad told me that he could remember feeling Mom's big belly when I used to kick inside there. I told him that I was just saying Hello!

Dad and I would always feel the baby kick. It feels real weird but I like it.

Mom and Dad went to special childbirth classes to help them learn about having another baby.

They always practiced at home for the time when the baby would come out. The time when the baby comes out is called labor.

Labor is very hard work for moms.

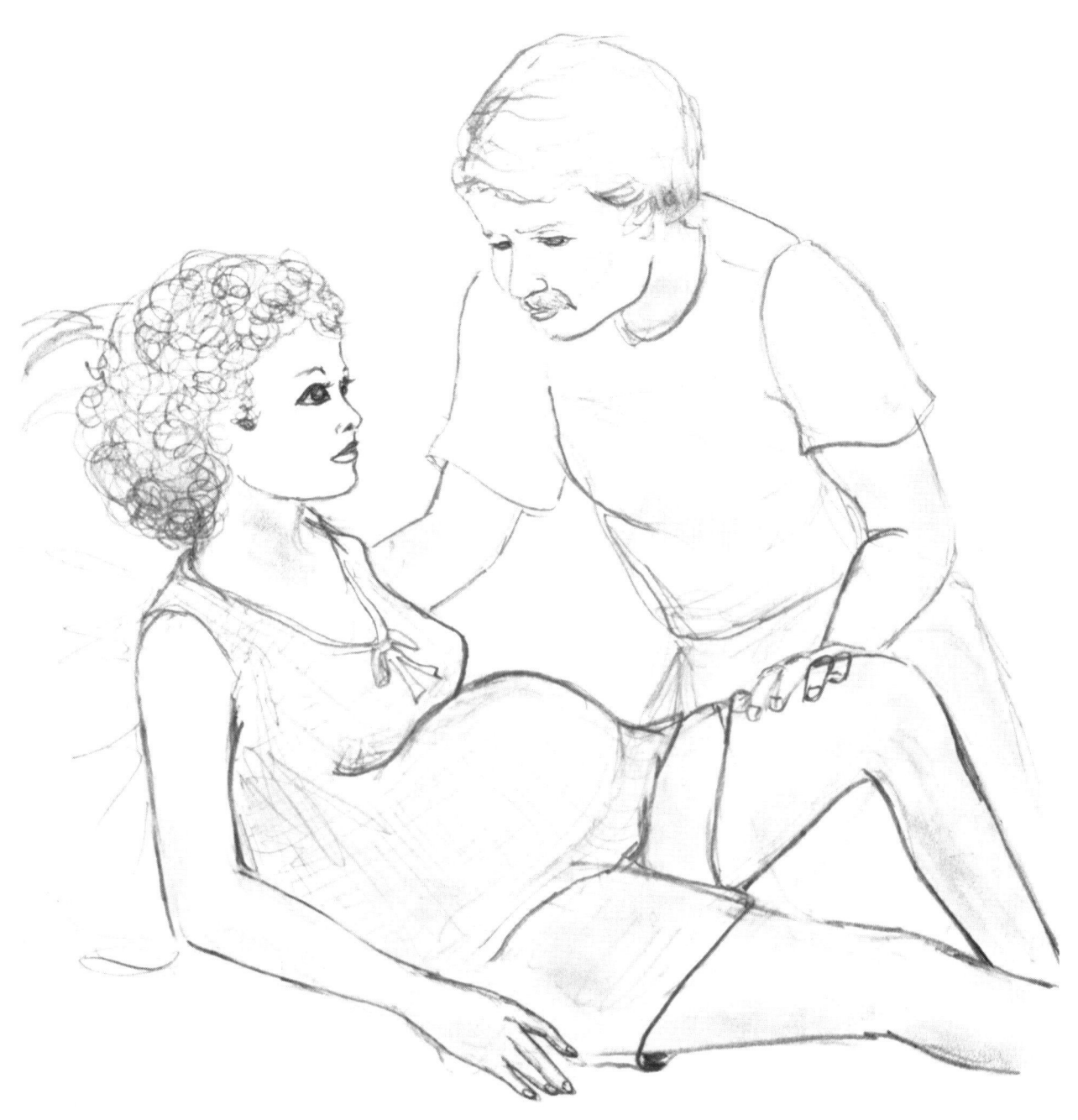

Dad and Mom went to special Childbirth Classes to help them learn about having another baby.

Mom showed me pictures in books about babies growing in moms' tummies and getting born. When babies are still inside they have long hoses attached to their belly buttons. This is how they get their food.

Mom says that's why everyone has a belly button. She also said that babies swim upside down in a whole bunch of water. That's a little bit hard to understand.

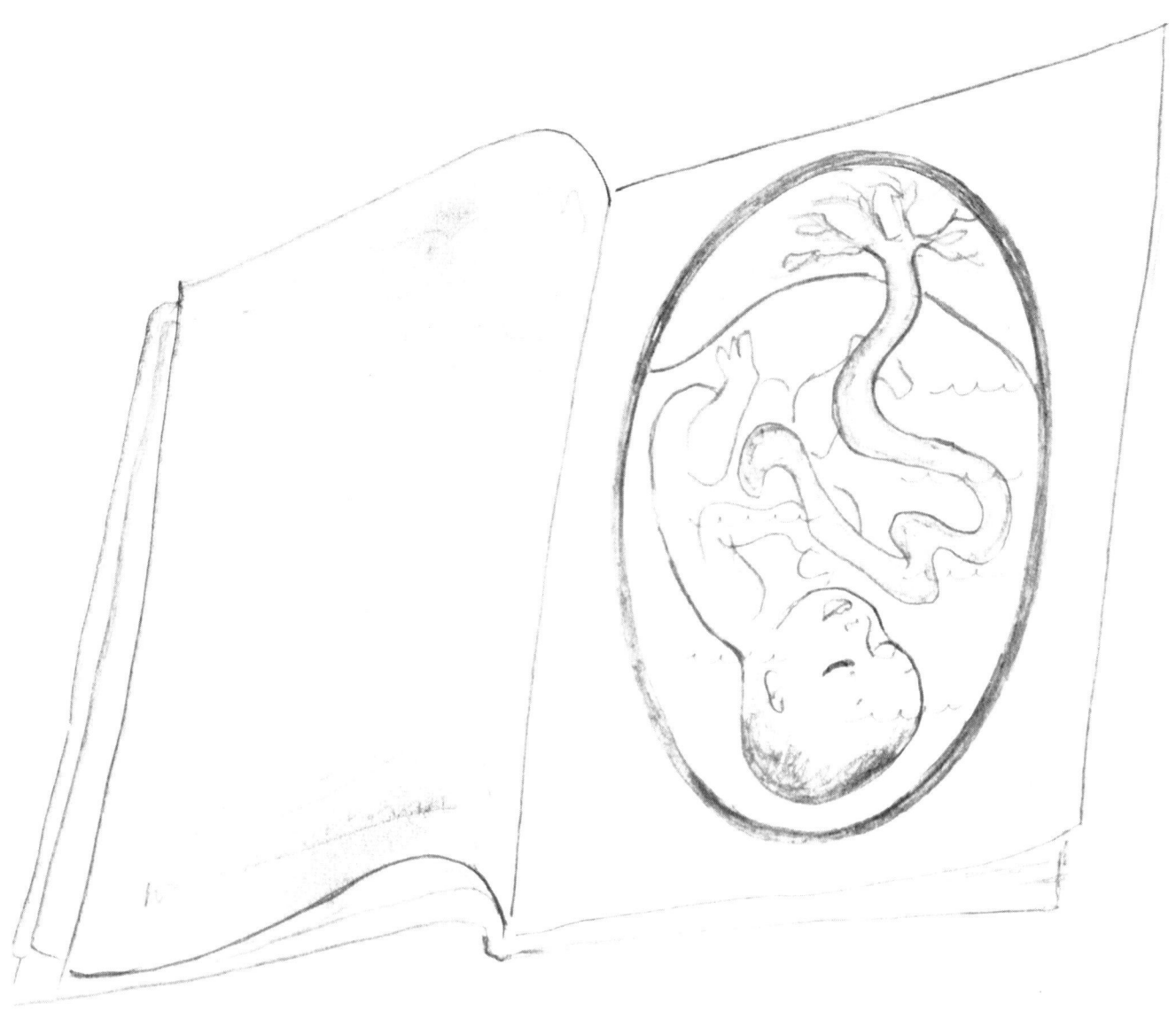

Mom showed me pictures of what the baby looked like inside of her tummy. He has a long food hose attached to his belly button.

When our baby grew big enough in Mom's tummy, Mom went into labor. Labor is hard work for mommies. Daddies, nurses, midwives and doctors have to help them.

My Daddy had to help my Mom a lot so that the baby could get born. Sometimes labor takes a few hours and sometimes it takes a whole day.

Mommies in labor often go away for a few days and they stay in the hospital with the baby. When their mommies go away, big kids usually get to stay with their Grandmas or their special friends until their mommy and new baby come home.

When the baby was big enough, Dad helped Mom to have the baby come out. This is called Labor.

When labor is over the baby is born. Then everyone is very happy. I was very happy!

That means that there will be a new baby in the house. That's very exciting. I never saw such a tiny new baby before. Her little eyes were wide open and everything. I didn't know that tiny little babies could see. She sure liked to look at Mom.

When labor is over, the baby comes out of Mom's tummy.
Isn't our baby girl cute?

Mom and Dad let me touch her and hold her. She was real hard to hold because her head was very wobbly and she couldn't sit up by herself. It's fun holding a new little baby, but it's also very hard work.

I kept telling her that she was my new little sister, but I don't think she could understand.

I'm happy to hold our new baby. Her head is wobbly and she's very hard to hold. She's too little to sit up by herself.

Tiny newborn babies can't talk at all, but they sure can make lots of neat funny faces. They must practice a lot before they are born. She makes me laugh sometimes.

My baby sister always makes a really big funny face when I try to kiss her. I think she hates it!

Her skin is so soft. I always like to touch it.

She makes lots of funny faces. Maybe she doesn't like it when I kiss her. Her face is very soft.

Big people are really crazy about little babies. They like to hold them, and talk to them and give them new presents.

My new little sister doesn't even know about presents - she doesn't even care - babies are sure strange.

She's even too little to open her presents. Mom and I always have to open them for her. That's fun!

Big people are really crazy about little babies. They like to hold them and give them lots of presents.

I hope that someone brings me a present! Presents always make me happy.

Mom says that when I was a baby I was given lots of presents too. I don't remember that. I want a present now, just like the baby!

I hope someone brings me a present. Presents make me very happy!

We have lots of visitors now that we have a new baby. Some of them bring pretty good food and fruit and cookies and stuff. That's pretty neat.

After they give Mom the food or presents, they ask to see the baby. Big kids are pretty special too, but no one fusses very much over me. Well, maybe Grandma does!

Everyone always likes to hold the baby. Mostly she doesn't care if people hold her. She just sits there.

Our baby doesn't care if people hold her. She just sits there. Everyone sure likes to hold her.

But I like it best when the visitors go home and we're all alone. We can do lots of fun things all by ourselves.

Now that the baby's out of Mom's tummy, there's room for me on her lap again. Now she can hold two babies. I'm just teasing, I'm not really a baby!

I'm glad when the visitors go home. I can sit on Mom's lap again now that the baby is out of her tummy.

Mom lets me help her to take care of the baby. Mom cleans her belly button where her long food hose used to be... newborn babies' belly buttons are a little bit weird!

Our new baby is too young to use the potty so she goes poop and everything in her diaper. Mom lets me help her change the diapers but I only like to help with the wet ones!

Mom lets me help her take care of the baby. She has a funny belly button. We have to change her diaper when she messes it.

Her little fingers and toes are so tiny and cute and pink. She always keeps her fingers closed tight in little fists. She's too little to hold anything yet. Not even one of her baby rattles.

    Mom says that the baby can wear a lot of clothes that I wore when I was a baby. I don't remember ever being that little!

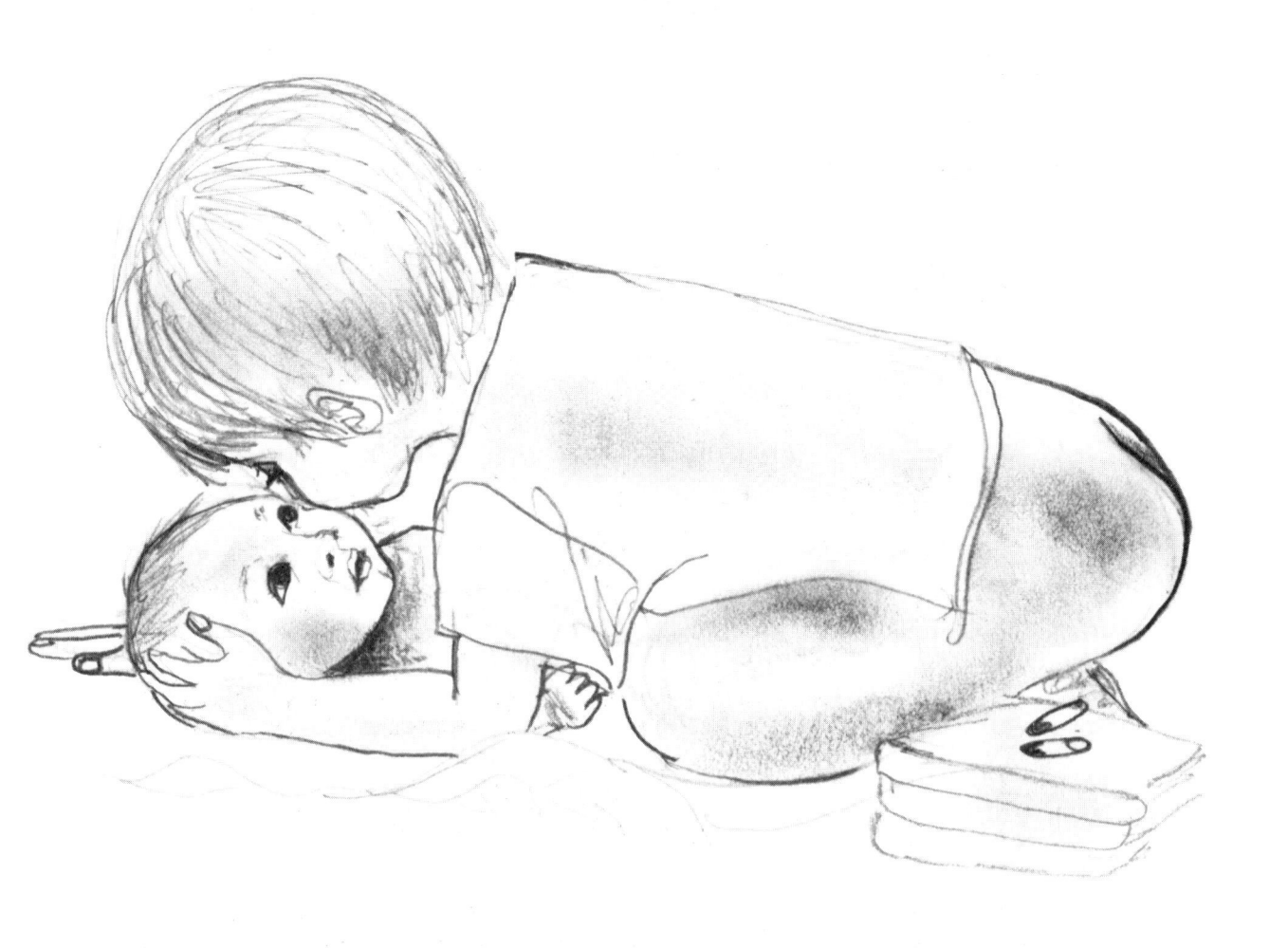

Our baby girl is so cute and tiny and pink and soft. It's fun to hold her and feel her skin. I sure am lucky to have a baby sister!

Babies are pretty lazy. They just lie there while you dress them.

They don't play with toys or anything. They just sleep and eat and lie around and sit in people's laps. They can't even go out to play.

Babies are lazy. They just lie around all of the time. They can't even go out to play!

I'm a big kid. I don't have to just lie around on a blanket. I can always help get myself dressed. I can play with toys.

On sunny days I can go outside and play with my friends. I can even ride my bike. Little babies can't do that!

I'm luckier than a baby. On sunny days I can go out and play on my bike.

Our baby doesn't eat regular food yet. She nurses. That means that she drinks milk from Mom's breasts. My new baby cousin drinks milk from a bottle. I drink milk from a cup!

Mom said that I used to nurse too when I was a baby -- I don't remember that. I wonder what Mom's milk tastes like. Hmm....

Our baby doesn't eat regular food. She drinks milk from Mom's breasts. Mom said that I used to nurse too. I wonder what Mom's milk tastes like.

Our baby nurses from Mom a lot. She nurses on the couch, in the rocking chair and in Mom and Dad's big bed.

I like to sit and watch her nurse. Sometimes I pat her head. Sometimes I let her hold my finger.

Mom says that nursing makes the baby happy and healthy. Mom smiles a lot when she nurses the baby, so I think it makes Mom happy and healthy too!

Mom is very happy when she nurses the baby.

After she finishes nursing, the baby sleeps. Our baby sleeps and sleeps and sleeps! I wish she would wake up so that I could hold her.

I wish she would wake up so that I could see her cute eyes and all her funny silly faces.

Our baby sleeps and sleeps and sleeps. I wish she would wake up so that I could see her cute eyes and funny faces.

Mom is very tired all of the time. She rests a lot. She says that having a baby is very hard work, so mommies and new babies must get lots of extra rest and take naps.

Sometimes we all nap together. It's fun to sleep with the baby. Sometimes at night we all sleep together. Even Daddy! I like that!

Mom says it's hard work to have a baby, so she and the baby take extra naps. I like to see the baby sleep with Mom. I like to sleep with Mom too!

Once in awhile when it's not nap time, I lie around in Mom's big bed with the baby.

I like the way the baby smells. She's real cuddly and it's fun to hug her. No wonder Mom holds her all the time!

Sometimes I nap with the baby too. Sometimes I just fool around with the baby when it's not nap time. Getting under the blankets with the baby is fun.

Once in awhile our new baby cries. I don't like it at all when she cries. It sounds terrible!

I ask Mom to nurse her or change her or rock her. I can rock her too!

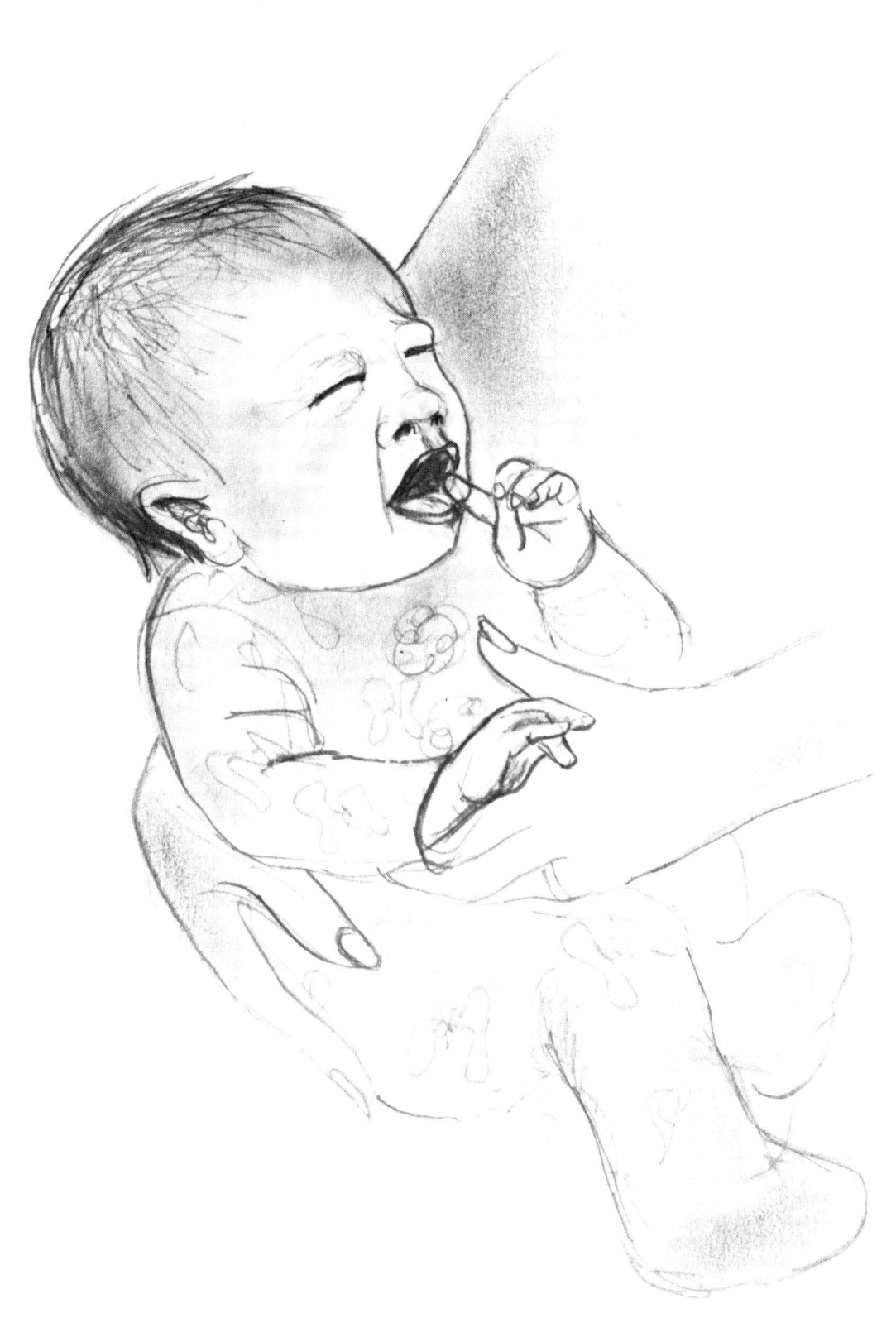

I hate when the baby cries. She makes a terrible sound. I ask Mom to nurse her or something.

Now that the new baby is here, Dad and I are doing some very special things together by ourselves.

Dad says that Mom needs some time alone with the baby so that they can get to know each other better. Just like she did with me when I was a baby.

Sometimes when Mom stays with the baby, Dad and I have special fun together.

While Mom rests, Dad and I do some house work. Dad vacuums the floor and I do the dishes. Doing the dishes is lots of fun.

We also fix some healthy food for Mom so that she can make good milk for the baby. That makes her happy.

Dad and I do housework while Mom rests. It's fun to do the dishes! We make food for Mom too.

When Dad and I are finished working around the house, we can play.

We play games, we blow bubbles. I'm pretty lucky to be a big kid and play these fun games with Dad. The baby is too little to play with us.

When Dad and I finish our work, we play again. The baby is too little to play with us. Maybe when she grows up, we can blow bubbles together.

I didn't remember too much about being a baby so Dad showed me my baby book. I saw lots of pictures of myself when I was a baby. Everyone was holding me and smiling at me. Just like they do with my baby sister!

    I'm glad that Dad showed that book to me. It was fun to see myself when I was a baby.

Dad showed me my baby book. It's a book all about me. It has lots of pictures of when I was a baby. It makes me feel special --- just like a little baby.

Sometimes I think it's more fun to be a baby than a big kid. Sometimes I pretend to be a baby. Babies get carried around. Babies get to sit in special chairs. Babies can wet their pants.

Dad says that sometimes big kids forget to go to the bathroom on time. He says that wet diapers are okay for babies, but that big kids have to try harder to use the potty.

I have to think about that!

Dad says it's okay for babies to wet their diapers but that big kids have to try hard to use the potty. I have to think about that!

The baby has lots of new fun things to play with, but she's too little to play with anything yet.

Mom and Dad let me play with her toys. But they say that I have to be careful with them and put them back when I'm finished. I'll let her play with my toys too when she gets big enough.

Mom and Dad let me play with the baby's new toys. They said I must put them away when I'm finished.

I'm a little sad that my baby sister is too small to play with me. My friends down the street have a baby too. But their baby is bigger and can laugh and play and crawl all around. Their baby plays PAT-A-CAKE and can even throw a ball.

My baby sister can just kick her legs and make silly faces. Mostly she just hangs around with Mom. Mom says that when our baby gets bigger she'll start to do more fun things, too. I can't wait!

I'm a little sad that my baby sister is too young to play with me. Mostly she just hangs around with Mom.
 I thought when the baby came that we could play games together, but she's just too little.

Mom holds our new baby a lot. She also nurses her a lot. She even smiles at her and kisses her a lot. Mom really loves our new little baby girl very much.

Mom kisses me too. Mom loves me a lot too. She told me!

Mom really loves our new baby very much. She holds her and kisses her and hugs her all of the time.
  Mom kisses me too!

Mom seems a little different now. Sometimes she is very, very happy. Sometimes she is very very sad. I even saw her cry once!

Sometimes when she's extra tired, she gets angry with me. Sometimes I get angry, too!

Sometimes Mom gets extra tired and she gets angry with me. Sometimes I get extra tired and I get angry too!

After Mom has some time alone with the baby and has had a good rest, she is very happy to see me.

While the baby is nursing or sleeping she reads a story to me. I love to hear stories.

When we have a good nap, we're not tired anymore. While the baby is still sleeping Mom reads a story to me.

At night when it's time to go to bed, sometimes we all snuggle together. Dad and Mom give me kisses and hugs. I pat my new baby sister's little head.
    I love my Mom and Dad. I love my new little baby sister!

Sometimes we all snuggle together. I love my Mom and Dad. I love my new little baby sister!

July, 1980

Dear Parent,

After reading this book to your child and experiencing the special interactions between your older child and the new baby, you may have some new ideas for this book.

If so, we would love to hear from you. Just send your ideas and any unique photos expressing these ideas to the publisher. Thank you!

Warmly,

Maryann Malecki
Pennypress
1100 23rd Ave. E.
Seattle, WA.
98112

IF YOU WOULD LIKE TO ORDER ADDITIONAL COPIES OF

Our Brand New Baby!

THE ORDER BLANKS BELOW.

ORDER FORM

ase send _____ copies of *We Have A Brand New Baby!* at $5.95 each, or $5.00 each 10 or more copies to:

NE. . . . .

DRESS. . . . .

Y. . . . . .STATE/PROVINCE. . . . . .ZIP. . . . .

check for_____(U.S. Funds) is enclosed. Washington State residents must 5.3% sales tax.

ORDER FORM

ase send _____ copies of *We Have A Brand New Baby!* at $5.95 each, or $5.00 each 10 or more copies to:

NE. . . . .

DRESS. . . . .

Y. . . . . .STATE/PROVINCE. . . . . .ZIP. . . . .

check for_____(U.S. Funds) is enclosed. Washington State residents must 5.3% sales tax.

"Our Brand New Baby! prepares a young child for many of the events surrounding the birth of a sibling — cially the realization that the new baby takes a great deal of Mother's time and is not really a playmate. The presents ways a child can help with a new baby and develop a feeling of closeness."
— Elizabeth Crary, parent educator and a of **Without Spanking or Spoiling**

Maryann has done it again! All the scenes from life with a newborn appear in a book of most appealing dra and commentary. After reading it with us, Cornelia, our 3-year-old, remarked, "Just like at our house."
— Tom Brewer, M.D., and Gail Brewer authors of **What Every Pregnant Wo Should Know About Diet and D During Pregnancy**

Maryann Powell Malecki is a Registered Nurse with a Bachelor of Arts Degree, having majored in Anthr ogy and minored in Child Psychology. She is certified by the American Society for Psychoprophylaxis in C trics, the Society for the Protection of the Unborn Through Nutrition, and is a La Leche League Leader. She the staff of the Childbirth Center of Daytona, Florida, where she is a nurse, nutrition counsellor, childbirth e tor, labor and birth assistant, and a breastfeeding counsellor. In her childbirth preparation classes, she cou parents on preparing their children for the arrival of a newborn sibling. In collecting material for **Our Brand Baby!** she utilized her and her husband's personal experiences as parents of four children, as well as the e ences of many other parents who kept diaries of their children's behavior and feelings when another chil born.

Maryann Malecki is also the author of **Mom and Dad and I Are Having A Baby!**

$5.95

ISBN 0-937604-